MW00877076

# Weekly Spiritual Practice:

## One Spiritual Practice for Each Week of the Year

Robert Flaherty

ISBN-13:978-1512390773

# DEDICATION

To Sandy for all her support and encouragement for this project
and so many other projects

# CONTENTS

# ACKNOWLEDGMENTS

No significant project happens in a vacuum. This one certainly didn't. I have to say thanks to all those who have been parishioners over my pastoral career of thirty-four years. They have let me practice teaching, writing, and now publishing these spiritual practices. Many have practiced these very practices and expressed gratitude and encouraged me to publish them.

The creative work of writing the practices is one thing. Publishing them is another. Marketing the published product is still another. I have to thank D'Anne Olsen, one of my faithful encouragers, for introducing me to Gail Watson, a local desk top publisher. D'Anne was giving me that gentle push to move my written words into published form. Gail turned me on to Create Space, an Amazon company. Create Space deserves my thanks, too. Without a publisher that makes self-publishing easy and inexpensive this book would never have come to print.

# Weekly Spiritual Practice

Two shaping influences immediately come to mind when I think about what brought me to write this collection of spiritual practices. The first is the example of a colleague. One of my assignments as an Army chaplain was with an aviation brigade during and after a period of combat in Iraq. Because there were so few Catholic chaplains in the Army, our brigade did not have a priest. Needless to say we had many Catholic Soldiers. That meant we had to borrow a priest from neighboring units. The nice thing about being in an aviation brigade is that we could fly him from one location to another. It was not uncommon for a priest to do five or more masses in one run.

I was lucky enough that sometimes my duty was to accompany my Catholic colleague. I noticed one priest in particular would ask a question at the end of his homily and encourage the soldiers to think about it during the week or he would give them some simple action to perform that was inspired by the gospel of the day. I considered what he was doing to be a form of group spiritual direction.

Over the years, I tried to incorporate this into my weekly sermons. In my current pastoral position, I have managed to do it every Sunday. I called the activities I was asking people to do "Spiritual Practices." I learned to use the word "practice" from Buddhist and Hindu friends, who so freely talked about practice. I also noticed that Buddhist and Hindu writers often included some practice, often meditation of some kind, in their writing. In fact, some of the revered holy texts include manuals of instruction in meditation.

Jewish and Christian scriptures offer minimal instruction with regard to specific practices. The disciples ask Jesus on one occasion to teach them to pray. He offers minimal instruction which consists primarily of a giving them a model prayer, "the Lord's prayer." In another place, Jesus instructs his disciples to pray in secret and not to attract attention to themselves when they do acts of piety. For the most part, the scriptures refer to spiritual practice with the assumption that the readers engage in the practice. So the writers of Scripture talk about prayer, fasting, ritual cleansing, acts of justice and so on without giving specific instruction how to perform the practice.

Spiritual directors and teachers in the Christian and Jewish tradition give specific instructions. Many practices they teach are similar to Eastern practices.

I found that these practical exercises, both from East and West, attracted me. I wanted not merely to know about my faith, but to put into practice; to do something. These exercise filled that need for me. I started to think about how I might share the way I was practicing with my congregation, and voila the weekly spiritual practice. Each week, at least in my mind, there is a connection between the scripture lesson that was the basis for my sermon and the spiritual practice. At first the connection to the scripture felt tighter. As the process continued to evolve for me, the themes of the scripture lesson became wider and consequently, it felt to me that the spiritual practices may not have been as closely tied to the scripture. Still, I was sharing practices that I had worked with.

I include the spiritual practice as part of my weekly sermon, print the practice in our worship bulletin, in our church newsletter, and on individual sheets that my administrative assistant posts in nine places throughout the church. Six of those places, by the way, are in the bathrooms. I get lots of interesting comments about that. I also publish the practices on my blog, on my Facebook page, and on Beliefnet.com. The feedback from parishioners and from friends and strangers alike who read the spiritual practices on line have encouraged me to continue writing a spiritual practice each week.

This book is the next step. I hope you will find these practices helpful and I invite you to share them with others.

## How to use this book

You will notice that there are fifty-two spiritual practices, theoretically one each week of the year. One way to use the book is to do one practice each week. You could do this individually or with a small group of friends.

If you choose to work with a group, you could go over the practice together then for the next week practice individually. When you meet the next week you could share your experience. Of course, with email, Twitter, Facebook, and other internet ways of connecting, you could share your experiences between meetings, too. You could agree to practice together for a whole year or choose a few to practice together for a specified number of weeks.

Another way to use the book is to choose selected practices. You could thumb through the book to find one or more practice that speak to you and try them. You don't have to confine yourself to only a week of practice. Some of the practices are so helpful that you may want to continue using until you feel the practice has lost its effectiveness for you. You can always come back and practice that way later in the year.

# Breathing Peace

You can use Thich Nhat Hanh's poem to practice peace.
*Breathing in, I calm body and mind.*
*Breathing out, I smile.*
*Dwelling in the present moment*
*I know this is the only moment.*
— Thich Nhat Hanh, *Being Peace*

Thich Nhat Hanh's poems are easily incorporated into mediation. You can start by following your breath. Follow your breathing, saying, "In" on the in breath and "Out" on the out breath. When you are ready you can repeat the words of the poem on the in and out breaths.

*On the in breath:* Breathing in, I calm body and mind.
*On the out breath:* Breathing out, I smile.
*On the in breath:* Dwelling in the present moment
*On the out breath*:   I know this is the only moment.

You can shorten the phrases if you wish, something like this:
Calm
Smile
Present moment
Only moment
You can practice at any time

- In your formal meditation time
- As you wait for soothing else, a stop light or an elevator, for example
- While you walk
- While you sit
- Just before you sleep

Breathe the poem several times each day.

# Confidently Use Your Gifts

You have been entrusted with gifts that only you have. Often people don't value their gifts, or think they aren't worth much, or for some other reason decide not to use their gifts thereby missing the chance to appreciate themselves or to be a blessing to others.

During this week confidently use your gifts for your good and for the good of others. At the end of the day celebrate the times you've used your gifts throughout the day. One way to celebrate your gift is simply to acknowledge it. You could keep a list in your journal for a few days. Complete these sentence stems:

Today I was aware of these gifts …

Today I used this gift [name the gift] to …

In order to help you recognize your gifts, listen for how others affirm your gifts. I have a friend who does this very well. After I have done something, often without recognizing that I stopped to do it, or have said something, or interacted with another person, he simply says, "Bob, that's your gift."

As a variation of this practice you could look for ways to affirm the gifts of your friends and family. As you notice them doing something helpful or meaningful, you could simply say to them, "That's your gift."

# Matthew 17:1-5

The story of Jesus' transfiguration is a favorite of mine. Here is Matthew's version of the story. The same story occurs in Mark and Luke.

*Six days later, Jesus took with him Peter and James and his brother John and led them up a high mountain, by themselves. And he was transfigured before them, and his face shone like the sun, and his clothes became dazzling white. ... Suddenly a bright cloud overshadowed them, and from the cloud a voice said, "This is my Son, the Beloved; with him I am well pleased; listen to him!"*

What especially attracts me to this story is that we normally think of Jesus in the various roles he fulfilled—teacher, healer, preacher. In the story of Jesus' transfiguration, the disciples saw him as pure light. They saw as it were the pure essence of being.

People have a way of defining us, too. They define us by what we do, who we are related to, what we accomplish or what we own. We are tempted to fall into the trap of identifying ourselves by the same measurements and we lose sight of the fact that just being makes us valuable. Use the following practice to appreciate being.

# Experience Transfiguration

What happens to you when you let go of the image you hold of yourself?

What happens when you let go of your thoughts or at least don't cling to them?

What happens when you simply observe?

This week practice letting go of your thoughts, images, and feelings and simply observe them without judgment. This may be a moment of transfiguration for you—a direct experience of being.

Chances are you will be aware when a thought or image arises. If you do nothing, sometime later you will be aware that you are no longer thinking that thought or seeing that image. In this practice, you are watching the thoughts and images arise and go away.

# Find God in All People

In 1998 I visited India. I made my visit as a world religions pilgrimage. I wanted to experience firsthand the religious pluralism of what I viewed as the most religiously diverse country in the world.

Gandhi appreciated the diversity of culture and religion in the country of his birth. Among many of the words of wisdom he left behind are these: "I am part and parcel of the whole and cannot find God apart from the rest of humanity."

Since returning to the United States, I have learned that I was mistaken about the most religiously diverse country in the world. It is not India, but the US. Diversity of culture and religion is all around us.

During this week, when you see people from different races and countries, on the street or on television, use it as a cue to say these words of Mahatma Gandhi as your mantra:

*I am part and parcel of the whole and cannot find God apart from the rest of humanity.*

Let yourself feel the truth of these words.

# Inner Ease Technique

You can use this technique to affirm self-love and to reduce stress.  It will be most helpful if you try to use this technique three times a day for the next week.  It takes only a minute or two.  There are three simple steps:

Step 1:  Place your hand over your heart.  This gesture in itself, according to researchers at Heart Math, releases the hormone oxytocin.

Step 2:  As you breathe, imagine your breath is coming in and out through the center of your heart.  This will drop you into your heart center, one of the energy centers of the Chakra system.

Step 3:  On the in breath imagine you are breathing in compassion, ease, and love.  Exhale normally.

Try it right now and notice the change in energy you experience. Do this exercise a couple of times each day.

You can also use this technique when you sense anxiety, fear, anger or any other stress producing emotion.

# Spiritual Lessons
# from Ordinary Things

Meister Eckhart often surprises us with a phrase. Here is one such surprise: "Isness is God." Everything that exists reveals to us something about God.

Jesus understood this. He used common, familiar, every-day things to describe life. Often his parables begin with the words, "the kingdom of God (or heaven) is like." I like to paraphrase that phrase by saying "life is like." Jesus used things like mustard seeds, leaven, pearls and treasures. To observe the common realm is to gain insight into the spiritual realm.

Common things can teach us. This practice gives you a chance to see what you can learn from common objects. For the next few days, each day try to observe one common thing. Think of at least one characteristic of the object. What does the object and characteristic teach you about life?

For example, when I first wrote these words, I was also knitting hats to give away. As knitted, I practiced by saying to myself, "Life is like this knitted hat, one stitch following another building a pattern and producing something useful."

# Praying the News

Often when I watch the news, I feel discouraged, frustrated, or even angry. I've found praying the news a helpful way to turn these negative feelings into something more useful.

During this week as you watch or listen to the news, pay attention to one or two articles about issues that are troubling to you. Each day pray with the news using these two questions:

- God of love, what would you have me learn?

- Merciful God, how can I offer your compassion?

Keep note of your insights as you pray the news with these questions.

## Matthew 25:31-39

*When the Son of Man comes in his glory, and all the angels with him, then he will sit on the throne of his glory. All the nations will be gathered before him, and he will separate people one from another as a shepherd separates the sheep from the goats, and he will put the sheep at his right hand and the goats at the left. Then the king will say to those at his right hand, "Come, you that are blessed by my Father, inherit the kingdom prepared for you from the foundation of the world; for I was hungry and you gave me food, I was thirsty and you gave me something to drink, I was a stranger and you welcomed me, I was naked and you gave me clothing, I was sick and you took care of me, I was in prison and you visited me." Then the righteous will answer him, "Lord, when was it that we saw you hungry and gave you food, or thirsty and gave you something to drink? And when was it that we saw you a stranger and welcomed you, or naked and gave you clothing? And when was it that we saw you sick or in prison and visited you?" And the king will answer them, "Truly I tell you, just as you did it to one of the least of these who are members of my family, you did it to me."*

# Serving Jesus in "The Least of These"

*Truly I tell you, just as you did it to one of the least of these who are members of my family, you did it to me.* —Jesus

For one day, without necessarily changing your routine, intentionally look around your community. Do you see any of the people Jesus referred to in in the gospel—the sick, the thirsty, the hungry, the imprisoned, the naked? When you see them do you see Jesus? How do you respond to these people?

# Prayerfully Place before God Your Fears and Hopes about the Future

Our fears often paralyze us. We hide them or hide from them, thinking they will go away. Hiding our fears only seems to empower them.

The Senoi people of Malaysia teach their children to face their fears in their dreams. So, for example, if a child reports that in the night a tiger was chasing him in his dream, the advice is this: if the tiger chases you tonight, don't wake up. Rather, turn around and face the tiger. As a rule, the tiger turns into a domestic cat when confronted this directly.

So this week, bring your fears into the open in your prayers. Lay them out in the open. This counter intuitive practice brings the surprise that facing our fears seems to diminish them.

Sometimes our hopes as well as fears paralyze us. You can use this same practice with your hopes. Bring them into your prayer consciousness. Watch what happens to your hopes as you do this over time.

# Matthew 1:18-21

*Mary had been engaged to Joseph, but before they lived together, she was found to be with child from the Holy Spirit. Her husband Joseph, being a righteous man and unwilling to expose her to public disgrace, planned to dismiss her quietly. But just when he had resolved to do this, an angel of the Lord appeared to him in a dream and said, "Joseph, son of David, do not be afraid to take Mary as your wife, for the child conceived in her is from the Holy Spirit. She will bear a son, and you are to name him Jesus, for he will save his people from their sins."*

In this gospel story, Joseph knows that he should marry Mary. He learns it from his dream. Three other times in the opening chapters of Matthew, people receive messages of guidance in a dream and one more dream of warning comes at the end of the gospel. The wise men dream that they should not report to Herod as he had asked them. Joseph dreams that he should take Mary and the baby to Egypt and later in a series of dreams he receives guidance to return, not to Judah but rather to Galilee, specifically to Nazareth. At the end of the gospel, Herod's wife has a troubling dream about the scheme to end Jesus' life.

# Listen to Your Dreams

Try this spiritual practice: pay attention to your dreams. At the very least when you go to bed, intend to remember your dream and in the morning write out the little fragments that you remember. If you want to get more involved with your dream, you might consider writing the dream as soon after you have it as possible. Most often you will wake up after a dream. Some people keep a pad by their bed or a recording device to make notes, write out the dream, or make an audio recording.

On the next page you will find a worksheet you can use to record your dream and reflect on it. The numbers suggest a sequence to follow. You can skip around to answer the parts in any order. When you are finished you can review your work on the dream.

# Working with Your Dream

| 1. Date: | 8. Dream Title: |
|---|---|
| 2. Write out the dream | |

| 3. What are some of the significant events of the previous day? |
|---|

| 4. Dream theme.  Complete this sentence.  This dream is about ... |
|---|

| 5. List objects, actions, and events |
|---|
| Mark the items that grab your attention. |
| Write whatever comes to your mind about each item on your list, starting with those that grabbed your attention. |

| 6. What insights do you gain from this dream? |
|---|

| 7. What is this dream telling you to do? |
|---|

## Luke 19:1-8

*Jesus entered Jericho and was passing through it. A man was there named Zacchaeus; he was a chief tax-collector and was rich. He was trying to see who Jesus was, but on account of the crowd he could not, because he was short in stature. So he ran ahead and climbed a sycamore tree to see him, because he was going to pass that way. When Jesus came to the place, he looked up and said to him, "Zacchaeus, hurry and come down; for I must stay at your house today."*

*So he hurried down and was happy to welcome him. All who saw it began to grumble and said, "He has gone to be the guest of one who is a sinner."*

*Zacchaeus stood there and said to the Lord, "Look, half of my possessions, Lord, I will give to the poor; and if I have defrauded anyone of anything, I will pay back four times as much."*

Zacchaeus is a model of a person who makes amends.

After meeting Jesus he said that if he had defrauded anyone, he would pay them back four times the amount.

Zacchaeus committed himself to take a brave step. He wanted to live in community. He wanted to live peacefully and in harmony. He was willing to make himself vulnerable for the sake of his Jesus-inspired vision of what was possible.

# Making Amends

Twelve step programs devote two steps to the process of making amends.

*Step 8: We made a list of all persons we had harmed, and became willing to make amends to them all.*

*Step 9: We made direct amends to such people wherever possible, except when to do so would injure them or others.*

These two steps make up the spiritual practice I am recommending for this week. Make your list, and then where it is possible make direct amends.

Sometimes it is not possible or it is unwise to make direct amends. For example, you cannot make direct amends to a person who is no longer living. Sometimes to make amends brings more destruction to the person. In such a case, it might be better not to make direct amends.

You can make indirect amends in several ways. You can behave differently toward the person you have offended. You can make amends to a person who is in effect a stand in for the person to whom you would like to make direct amends. For instance, suppose you have injured your neighbor's dog. Then the neighbor moves and subsequently dies. You can treat another dog in a kind way. So, another way is that you can make indirect amends is to behave differently in similar situations.

**CAUTION:** Because this practice is fraught with potential hazards, I recommend you do this practice under the guidance of a spiritual director, counselor, or a trusted person who has done this practice.

# Ask, "Is it True?"

We constantly tell ourselves stories. The stories are sometimes fully developed, other times only a sentence. Often we take one or two "facts," things that are verifiably true, and weave them together with details, which may or may not be verifiable, to make a complete story. In other words, our life stories are a combination of fact and fiction.

In any case, our stories tell us who we are and where we fit in various relationships. Our stories indicate value and worth. You know the stories.

From our stories, we often draw conclusions—one sentence conclusions that begin like this, "I always do that because ..." or, "I'm so ..."

During this week, listen to the stories you tell yourself. Then ask, "Is it true?" You'll find that simply asking the question allows you to decide whether you want to continue telling that story or to change it. And, if you find yourself saying, "No, that isn't true," you will likely discover that the power of the story diminishes.

# Luke 14:16-22

*Then Jesus said to him, 'Someone gave a great dinner and invited many. At the time for the dinner he sent his slave to say to those who had been invited, "Come; for everything is ready now." But they all alike began to make excuses. The first said to him, "I have bought a piece of land, and I must go out and see it; please accept my apologies." Another said, "I have bought five yoke of oxen, and I am going to try them out; please accept my apologies." Another said, "I have just been married, and therefore I cannot come." So the slave returned and reported this to his master. Then the owner of the house became angry and said to his slave, "Go out at once into the streets and lanes of the town and bring in the poor, the crippled, the blind, and the lame." And the slave said, "Sir, what you ordered has been done, and there is still room."*

# Attend the Party

Jesus told a parable about a man who threw a big party. It was a wedding banquet. The host invited many guests, but they were too busy to come. They were so busy doing important things, making a living, caring for their families, managing their estates that they missed the party.

You've been invited to a great party—Life! You don't want to miss this party.

Before you go to bed this evening make a list of five things you could do tomorrow that would bring you joy. Your list is your invitation to the party. At the end of the day check your list. How many of those things did you do? Were there things that prevented you from doing them? Did you miss the party because you got too busy doing legitimate things?

# Be a Spirit Watcher

*The wind blows where it chooses, and you hear the sound of it, but you do not know where it comes from or where it goes. So it is with everyone who is born of the Spirit.*—Jesus

The poet and doctor William Carlos Williams used to carry a notepad around with him in which he listed "Things I noticed today that I've missed until today."

Make his practice into an ongoing project in your home or among friends. Every morning, remind yourself that during the day you are going to notice something new or see a familiar sight in a new way. In the evening, describe your discovery to family or friends or write it in your journal.

As you make these observations, do you see evidence of Spirit's presence? Happy Spirit watching.

# Challenge Limiting Beliefs

From the time of our entry into this life up until this present moment we are bombarded by messages that shape our lives. Some of the messages tell us about the nature of reality. Others teach us values. Still others tell us about ourselves. Some of these messages are encouraging. They motivate us to be the best we can be. Many other messages impose limits or curtail our full potential.

An art teacher observed that if you ask a group of preschool children if they are artistic, about eighty percent of the children will raise their hands affirming that they are artistic. If you ask a room full of middle schoolers the same question, less than ten percent of the class will claim their artistic abilities. This art teacher concluded that from preschool to middle school children are told repeatedly that they are not artistic or their art projects do not measure up to some standard. This kind of message puts limits on us.

Beware of your old conditioning and limitations family or friends may have imposed on you. When you hear a nagging little voice inside your head telling you that you can't do something, ask, "Who told you that?" And ask, "Is that true?" Asking these two questions will often free you from limiting beliefs.

A wonderful world of total possibility surrounds you. You can achieve remarkable things when you believe you can! You are an amazing person when you believe you are!

# Give Thanks

*If the only prayer you ever say in your entire life is thank you, it will be enough.* –Meister Eckhart

The evangelist Luke tells a story about Jesus cleansing ten lepers. Only one person returned to give thanks. This week give thanks using one or more of these steps:

Sometime during the day, morning before everything gets going or evening when things have slowed down are probably the best times, write a list of the things you are truly grateful for.

Look for opportunities to say thank you.

Pay attention to the number of times you say thanks. Each time you do, think of it as a prayer no matter to whom you have said, "Thank you."

I made these suggestions as part of a sermon. It was an awesome experience to hear people say thank you to me after worship and realize they were saying a prayer.

# Give up Worries

Do you worry? What do you worry about? Generally, people worry about what might happen. In other words, worry comes about because one is facing uncertainty. It follows then that if you can learn to live with uncertainty, can learn to take a wait-and-see-what-happens-and-then-I'll-respond attitude, worry will disappear. So how can you put away worries? Here are three strategies for letting go of worry.

Find a symbol to which you can give your worries. In Guatemala people use little worry dolls. They tell one of the dolls their concern and then at night put the worry doll under their pillow and let the doll worry about their concern while they sleep restfully. You could use a worry doll or another symbol to give your worries to.

Write your worries. Some folks find it helpful to write them in a journal and then close the book. Others find it helpful to write their worries and then shred the paper or burn it. This is a symbolic way to tell yourself you are letting go of your worries.

You can symbolically put them in a worry box. You can do this in your imagination or write your concern and put the paper into a box. In any case, you can then put the box on a shelf to take them up later, at a time of your choosing. Often you'll find it unnecessary to take them up.

Putting aside your worries about the future gives you the opportunity to live in the present moment, to enjoy it to the fullest.

# Matthew 25:1-13

*Then the kingdom of heaven will be like this. Ten bridesmaids took their lamps and went to meet the bridegroom. Five of them were foolish, and five were wise. When the foolish took their lamps, they took no oil with them; but the wise took flasks of oil with their lamps. As the bridegroom was delayed, all of them became drowsy and slept.*

*But at midnight there was a shout, "Look! Here is the bridegroom! Come out to meet him." Then all those bridesmaids got up and trimmed their lamps. The foolish said to the wise, "Give us some of your oil, for our lamps are going out."*

*But the wise replied, "No! there will not be enough for you and for us; you had better go to the dealers and buy some for yourselves."*

*And while they went to buy it, the bridegroom came, and those who were ready went with him into the wedding banquet; and the door was shut. Later the other bridesmaids came also, saying, "Lord, lord, open to us."*

*But he replied, "Truly I tell you, I do not know you." Keep awake therefore, for you know neither the day nor the hour.*

This parable, like so many Jesus tells, includes the phrase "The kingdom of heaven will be like …." Since the word "kingdom" sets up certain religious connotations, I like to make the phrase more universal, "Life is like this …" This paraphrase immediately raises two questions: how is life like this? And, more specifically, how is my life like this?

# Accept the Wise
# and Foolish Parts of Yourself

Jesus told a parable about ten bridesmaids. He called five of them wise and five foolish.

If wise ones and foolish ones characterize all of life, so too wise and foolish characterize each of us. What parts of you are wise? What parts are foolish? How do they fit together?

In your journal or in the quietness of your thoughts, answer each of the above questions. Can you accept both the wise and foolish aspects of yourself and integrate both into the picture you hold of yourself?

# Build your Support System

Human beings are made for community. We draw support from one another. Actually, we need several different kinds of support: Listeners, challengers, and encouragers. Consider who offers you support in each of the following categories:

| Support Category | Who offers this support? |
| --- | --- |
| **Listener:** one who simply listens to you without judgment | |
| **Work challenger:** one who is willing to tell you when you could have done a better job | |
| **Emotional challenger:** one who is willing to encourage you to find a better emotional frame of reference | |
| **Work encourager:** one who will cheer you on to bring out your best performance | |
| **Emotional encourager:** one who will affirm and encourage you that your feelings are appropriate to the situation | |

You may want to add two columns to the matrix: 1) How satisfied are you with this support? 2) What action do you want to take to strengthen this support? These additional columns will give you a way to evaluate your support system. If you are not satisfied you can take steps to strengthen your support system.

# Imagine Living Water

*The water that I will give will become in them
a spring of water gushing up to eternal life.*
—Jesus

Water is one image of Spirit or of Life. In this spiritual practice, I am suggesting a meditation on water to let you feel your connectedness with life.

Find a quiet place where you can be still. When you quiet yourself, close your eyes. Relax. Take a deep breath. Relax. Bring your attention to your feelings. Of what feeling are you most aware?

Now associate that feeling with water. Imagine your picture of water inside you expressing your feeling.

Project yourself into different parts of the day ahead of you or of yesterday. Bring your attention to the feelings stirred up by those different events. Again, associate your feelings with water. Does the image of the water change?

For some folks the water is a pond or a lake. In those instances the emotions are gentle or calm. For others, the water is a water fall, a spring, a brook, even a raging river. Each of those images suggests a different kind of feeling. Use this meditation practice to contact the emotions within—the springs of living water, life itself.

# Lectio Divina

Lectio Divina, Latin for divine reading, is a way to prayerfully read scripture. Read the passage three times. You can use any passage. One may immediately come to mind. I have suggested three. You could use any one of them or more than one for this practice. I learned to do Lectio Divina with passages from the Bible. I have found that the process works for any passage. Here are the three passages I have selected that you could use to try this practice: Matthew 25:31-46, Jesus' story of sheep and goats; John 5:2-9, a healing story; and an epistle reading, Ephesians 2:11-22.

At the first reading, simply listen to the words. Pause after reading for a few moments of silence. Simply let your thoughts, feelings and images percolate through the passage.

At the second reading, look for a word or phrase that speaks to you. Sit quietly with the word for a few minutes.

At the third reading, ask if the passage is asking you to do something. Sometimes you'll answer yes; other times, no. If it is asking you to do something pay attention to what it is asking. Is the passage in any other way speaking to you, offering you a word or encouragement or a word of challenge perhaps?

If you have the opportunity to do this with another person, you can share your responses with each other after each reading. If you do it alone, you can write your responses in your journal or simply take mental notes. The advantage of writing is that you can review the word or phrase, question and direction for action at the end of the day or the end of the week.

# Meditating with an Inspirational Passage

Even though there are probably more ways to meditate than there are meditation teachers, I'll offer a suggestion here.

Find a place where you can sit quietly. You can sit in lotus position, traditional Japanese Seiza posture, or sit in a straight backed chair. In any case, sit so your spine is straight and you can breathe freely. When you have quieted yourself, slowly repeat the words of an inspirational passage. If the passage is too long for you to memorize, simply have it available to read slowly. When you come to the end of the passage, repeat it. Fifteen to twenty minutes is enough. Some people like to do a session in the morning and another in the evening. One or the other is good, too.

You can pick your own passage or you can start with this verse: Do not conform to the pattern of this world, but be transformed by the renewing of your mind (Romans 12:2).

St. Francis prayer is also an excellent passage to use with this meditation technique.

*Lord, make me an instrument of thy peace.*
*Where there is hatred, let me sow love.*
*Where there is injury, pardon;*
*Where there is doubt, faith;*
*Where there is despair, hope;*
*Where there is darkness, light;*
*Where there is sadness, joy.*

*O Divine Master,*
*Grant that I may not so much seek*
*To be consoled as to console;*
*To be understood as to understand;*
*To be loved as to love.*

*It is in giving that we receive;*
*It is in pardoning that we are pardoned;*
*It is in dying that we are born to eternal life.*

*—Prayer of St. Francis*

# Remember: You Are the Light of the World

*You are the light of the world*—Matthew 5:14

These words are in the collection of Jesus' teaching called the Sermon on the Mount. They make a wonderful affirmation. I'm suggesting that you say these words to yourself several times during the day. One particularly powerful way to repeat them is to say them to yourself while you are looking at yourself in a mirror. You can incorporate this practice into your morning routine. Look yourself in the eye and call yourself by name and say, "You are the light of the world."

Then during the day repeat these words to yourself. No doubt, there will be times in the day when you find it relatively easy to say this. Those are the times when you feel good about yourself or you are aware of your positive influence. No doubt, there will also be times in the day that you might find it difficult to repeat these words. In fact, that little nagging voice in the back of your head might add, "you got to be kidding." You might be tempted to ignore the affirmation at that moment. That is the moment you are tempted, as Jesus put it, to put your light under a bushel. At that moment remind yourself, no matter what it looks or feels like, "You are the light of the world."

# Remembering God's Presence

*In order to know God, we must often think of Him.*
–Brother Lawrence

In his farewell speech to his disciples, Jesus promised his followers that, they would know the Spirit of truth "because he abides with you, and he will be in you." John 14:17. The practice for this week is to remember that the Spirit is with you and in you. Here is one way to practice.

Think of some repetitive action or event that happens throughout your day—like the ringing telephone, commercials on TV, turning on a water spigot, stopping at a stop sign or red light. Every time the event occurs let it be a reminder for you to pause and say to yourself, "The Spirit of truth is with me and in me."

# See the World in a Different Way

A traditional morning prayer includes these words, "New every morning is your love, great God of light." Often we get caught in thinking the world or at least our experience of it is repetitive or down right boring. This practice encourages you to experience the freshness of each moment.

Take a few minutes at the beginning of your day to quiet yourself and then say to yourself, "There is a different way to see* the world." You can bring to mind specific situations and say "There is a different way to see this." Throughout the day, as you face situations that hook you, take a few seconds to withdraw from that situation and say again to yourself, "There is a different way to see this."

*You could substitute "hear," "feel," or "experience" for "see."

# Signs of Life

Traditional words of committal at a graveside include these: "while we are in life we are in death." One could turn these words around with equal veracity. While we are in death we are in life. The distinction between the two is likely not as rigid as we think. And one likely contains the other, or at least seeds of the other.

The evangelist John tells a story about one of Jesus' friends, Lazarus, who had just died. Jesus and his disciples leave the place where they were staying to go to Bethany, Lazarus' home town. Lazarus was already in the burial tomb. Martha one of Lazarus' sisters heard that Jesus was on the way. She went out to meet him. They have a conversation about Lazarus, Jesus' absence at the time of his death, and resurrection. In the course of conversation—picture this at the grave side of Lazarus—Jesus tells Martha, "I am the resurrection and the life." He says this while she is grieving her brother's death. Then he has the audacity to add, "Do you believe this?" He asks her to believe the unbelievable. Or is it really? Here is recognition that while we are in death we are in life.

This brings me to the spiritual practice: recognizing life in the midst of death. What is the worst thing that is happening or about to happen in your life? That's death. It doesn't take long to bring this event to mind. What would the solution look like? Or what is the strength I need to go on? That is life. Once you imagine the solution ask yourself, "how is that solution or at least parts of it manifesting right now?" Or, "how is the strength to go on already present?"

Look for the signs of life manifesting even in the midst of death.

# Enjoy Each Meal

As Luke tells the gospel story, at least ten of the vignettes of Jesus' life occur in the context of a meal and several other stories draw on imagery of a meal or food. Mealtime conversations become occasions to teach, to share life, to reflect. For Jesus, his disciples, and for us mealtimes connect us with each other.

Bless each meal you eat this week with awareness. Be aware of the food itself, of all those whose effort went into bringing food to your table, of all the elements that went into the production of the food, of the people who share the meal with you, of your connection to all of life.

# Tonglen

Tonglen is a Tibetan Buddhist practice. In the practice, one visualizes taking into oneself the suffering of others on the in-breath, and giving happiness and wellbeing on the out-breath.

Imagine an instance of suffering, maybe something you saw on the news or read, like floods in the mid-section of the country, or maybe you see someone as you pass them on the street or in the mall. On your in-breath you imagine you are taking in their suffering. Then when you breathe out, you imagine that you are transmitting peace, happiness and wellbeing to them.

Usually tonglen is practiced on behalf of other people. There are other practices to use on your own suffering. Nonetheless, you could modify the tonglen practice to breathe wellbeing into your own life. So, if you are suffering, you could pick an image which represents your pain and breathe it in. On the out breath you could imagine the breath of peace and wellbeing spreading over your being.

Your connection to other people may come through your own suffering. If you are experiencing a particular hardship, you can use this practice to recognize that you are not alone. No doubt out of the seven billion of us on the planet, there are other people who are experience similar hardship. In your meditation, you can be aware of your suffering. You can take into your suffering the suffering of others. You can breathe out release from this suffering for yourself and for all who suffer with you. Tonglen is the practice of taking in suffering, your own and others, on the in breath, transforming it in that moment when you are neither breathing in nor out, and sending out peace on the out breath.

# Try on Something New

*Clothe yourselves with the new self,
created according to the likeness of God
in true righteousness and holiness.*
–Ephesians 4:24

Throughout my life I've lived in many different places. Early on in those moves I recognized that a move gave me the opportunity to start over. I could leave old behaviors in the old location and start over. The people I met never questioned me. I think they just assumed that's the way I had always been.

I know that when I have met people in these new locations, I simply assumed that what I experienced of them was an extension of their past. I have often been surprised when someone has told me about a past that is much different than what I was experiencing of them in the present. These experiences reinforced what I had learned in my many moves. If I present myself in a certain way, for the most part, people are willing to accept me that way.

Would a different attitude help you? Would acting a different way change how you feel about yourself? Would you like to react differently in a relationship? You can. For at least one day this week try it out as if you are putting on a different set of clothes. Try a new way of relating. Try a new attitude. After wearing the change for a day or so ask yourself how you feel.

# What If ...

*Do not be conformed to this world,*
*but be transformed by the renewing of your minds*
—Romans 12:2

Jesus saw a different world. "My kingdom is not of this world," he said. His kingdom had a different structure of power. In this world, those who hold power are the rulers. They lord it over their subjects. Not so in his kingdom. If you want to be great in his kingdom, be servant of all. In this world, riches are measured in the accumulation of possessions and wealth. In Jesus' kingdom, the one who wants to be rich gives it all away and in the process stores up treasures in heaven. In his kingdom there is a different pecking order. The first shall be last and the last shall be first.

For this week, take any one of Jesus different perceptions and play what if. It works something like this. In the morning say to yourself—maybe even out loud—what if the first shall be last? Then during the day pay attention to the events of the day as they unfold. You'll be surprised how many times in the day it becomes clear to you that the world lives in a different order than Jesus. I think you'll also be surprised 1) at the number of times you can put Jesus' value into practice and 2) at the number of times you find that something occurs that demonstrates Jesus' value.

# Light

Light is a significant element in the religions of the world, especially in their mystic traditions. Light often is a manifestation of the transcendent.

In the Christian tradition, John refers to "the true light, which enlightens everyone." The evangelists—Matthew, Mark and Luke—each tell the story of Jesus' transfiguration. In that story the way people generally perceived Jesus dropped away. That is they usually saw him filling a role, teacher, preacher, healer. In the transfiguration story, those fall away. His most intimate disciples see his essence, pure energy.

I would expect to hear a story likely to come out of an Eastern religious context. And, in fact, one can find such stories. The Buddha, for instance, is said to have been twice transfigured, at the moment of his enlightenment and at the moment of his death. Also in Hinduism there are stories of various sadhus who manifest as light.

The relationship of light and matter is described in scientific terms today. Albert Einstein, for instance, referred to matter as "only stopped light." In the structure of an atom, electrons have a natural orbit. If by an outside means one energizes an atom, the elections change their orbit. When the electron falls back to its normal orbit it emits a packet of energy, a photon or a bundle of light. The mystics and scientists sound like they are speaking the same language: light manifests as matter.

The pure essence of Jesus is our essence, too, whether we have the opportunity to see it or not.

# Witness the Light

During this week take a couple of times to meditate on the significance of light.

One way to do that is to light a candle and watch it burn for a few minutes. Another is to look at the stars at night. Light is all around. You can find other times this week to witness light.

Let your mind make its own connections to your experience of light and how you are light in the world.

# Who Am I?

Often our sense of self, of who we are, comes from outside. We often think of ourselves in terms of what we do or what we have accomplished; sometimes by what we have been able to accumulate or own; and still other times by what other people say about us.

Here's an exercise to help you discover some of the outside influences. During the day take note of what others say about you. It may be helpful to write down the comments.

Also pay attention to what you say about yourself. Again, writing may be helpful. At some time during the day, ask yourself, "Where did that come from?" Or, a variation, "Who says?"

Then as a follow on, ask yourself whether the comment is really you. Hint, more often than not, even if the comment is true, it is not really you and certainly not the whole of you.

# Ho'oponopono

Dr. Ihaleakala Hew Len, a therapist in Hawaii, worked with patients who were labeled "criminally insane." As he reviewed their files, he felt that he contributed to their condition. He began to say repeatedly, "I'm sorry. Please forgive me. I love you." Amazingly his patients, whom he never even saw, demonstrated remarkable improvement.

Hew Len's practice has roots in Hawaiian culture. When people had difficulties, personal, relational, emotional, they sought the help of the shaman who helped them perform a mental cleansing. The cleansing involved accepting their involvement in their situation and seeking forgiveness. Dr. Hew Len adapted this practice in his therapeutic work at the prison. The practice is known in Hawaiian as ho'oponopono.

# Ho'oponopono Practice

A simple practice for healing and reconciliation comes from Hawaii. One finds variations in other Polynesian cultures.

Repeat these words often during the day. You can repeat them without a context or you can place them in a context by bringing to mind a specific person or a particular setting.

I'm sorry.

Please forgive me.

Thank you.

I love you.

# What if (Up)

We regularly play the What-if game. You start asking yourself what if this? What if that? Before long "what if" disappears and you are certain that this or that is the reality of your life. Unfortunately, most of the time we play What-if (Down). This or that is something we worry about. For example, what if the market crashes and my retirement fund won't support me? What if this cough turns out to be life threatening pneumonia? What starts out as a question of some possibility often turns into a statement of certainty. "The market will crash and my retirement fund won't support me," for instance.

This week, I'm encouraging you to play What-if (Up). What if I come into a lot of money? What if I win a trip around the world? Be as adventurous as you wish. These questions also suggest some possibility. More often than not we dismiss them as wishful thinking or fantasy.

Play with the what if (up) this week. Let the question of possibility turn into certainty, at least in your imagination. The up possibilities are as likely to be certain as the down what ifs. The downers pull you down emotionally and spiritually.

As you play with what if (up), notice what happens to the way you feel.

# Keep a Journal

Keeping a journal, a record of events of the day, both the external events and the internal ones, can be a very helpful experience. It is a relatively easy thing to keep a record of the external things—what happened during the day, who you talked with, the weather and so on. Sometimes it is not so easy to be aware of the internal events. Here are four questions to help you focus within. You might answer one each day or all four each day for several days.

- What was the best part of the day?

- What was the worst part of the day?

- What are you looking forward to tomorrow?

- What are you worried about tomorrow?

# Just Be

During this week practice this meditation. Simply say one line at a time. Pause between lines allowing the message to wash over you.

Be still and know that I am God.

Be still and know that I am.

Be still and know.

Be still.

Be.

# Just Like Me

Use the phrase "just like me" to signify your unity with others. Whenever you find yourself making an assessment of another person, whether you are saying something critical or something complimentary, right after you think or say it, add the statement "just like me." For example, "My partner is so stubborn, just like me." "My friend is so generous with her time, just like me." "She holds too many grudges, just like me." "He is so creative, just like me."

# Affirm Your Worth

Here are four things you can do every day to affirm your value (notice none of them have to do with money.)

- While you are looking at yourself in a mirror give yourself a compliment.

- Learn to accept compliments from others. Take note of what they say. Simply say, "thank you" to the person offering you the compliment.

- Say affirming things to yourself, like "I love YOU," "I am worthy," "I am enough," "I am a beloved child of God."

- Do something that you naturally do really well. Notice how you feel when you do it.

# Luke 18:10-14

Jesus told this story:

*Two men went up to the temple to pray, one a Pharisee and the other a tax collector. The Pharisee, standing by himself, was praying thus, 'God, I thank you that I am not like other people: thieves, rogues, adulterers, or even like this tax collector. I fast twice a week; I give a tenth of all my income.' But the tax collector, standing far off, would not even look up to heaven, but was beating his breast and saying, 'God, be merciful to me, a sinner!' I tell you, this man went down to his home justified rather than the other.*

In this story we often think "justified" refers to a relationship between God and the tax collector. While that is an obvious interpretation, I also like to think of the implications if one understands "justified" to mean "congruent." The tax collector accepts himself, weaknesses and all, for who he is.

Our society conditions us to live incongruently. We are encouraged to keep our image looking good. That means we are encouraged often to hide or deny our weaknesses. In fact, I think this is the lens through which we read the above parable. We have a tendency to disrespect the Pharisee, because we immediately see that he was protecting his image. The parable commends to us the one who acknowledged his weaknesses, his shadow side, his shortcomings.

The following practice gives you a way to acknowledge your shadow side and at the same time to let it go so that it does not have to control you.

# Loving Acceptance of Yourself

This spiritual practice is a breathing meditation. As you quiet yourself, follow your breath and then begin to say these words. As much as possible feel yourself offering acceptance to yourself.

[On the in breath] I am aware of disappointment in myself.

[On the out breath] I lovingly accept this part of myself.

I let this disappointment go.

I watch it leave.

This present moment.

This is the only moment.

You can become more specific than simply saying "disappointment in myself." You can name specifically your disappointment. For example, "I am aware that I lied to my friend."

# My Face in the Shrine

When I was in Japan, I took the opportunity to visit Shinto shrines. They are everywhere. Some are magnificent edifices. Others are a little box on a fence post in front of someone's house. Structurally they are very similar whether they are massive or tiny. In the center of the shrine, the holy place, is some representation of spirit. It could be an animal, a person, or a thing. A very common thing in this holy place is a mirror. When I first encountered a mirror in the holy place, the holy image I saw the in the shrine was my own face!

Later I learned that the mirror represents a mirror to reflect light which according to a sacred story Amaterasu, a primary Shinto *kami* or spirit, hid from her brother and consequently from everyone. She was coaxed into bringing the light out of the hiding place, thus blessing everyone with this great light.

In the spiritual practice that follows you can use a mirror to gaze at a holy child of God.

# Beloved Child of God

Each time you see your reflection in a mirror this week, and likely you will be surprised how many times you see yourself, pause long enough to really see yourself. Then say to that image in the mirror addressing the face by name, "[Your name], you are a beloved child of God."

# A Rich Man and Lazarus

One of Jesus' familiar stories can be read as an encounter with a "consequential stranger."[1] A consequential stranger is a person you meet in passing, perhaps a clerk at the grocery store, or the person in the line behind you, or a barista. You assume they are of no particular significance to you. Then later, you come to realize that person has made a significant contribution to your life. Maybe they have recommended you for a job or given you a helpful piece of advice. The person you thought you could simply dismiss as inconsequential turns out to have been a consequential stranger.

Here is Jesus' story. Lazarus, a beggar, sat at the gate of a rich man. The rich man had no time for Lazarus. Then they both died. Lazarus went to heaven; the rich man to hell. From his place of torment the rich man asked Abraham (the New Testament's version of the contemporary St. Peter who guards the gate of heaven in our stories about the afterlife) to have Lazarus give him just a drop of water.

"Can't be done," is Abraham's reply. The rich man makes a second request, "Send Lazarus back to warn my brothers to behave differently toward beggars." All of a sudden the rich man realized that Lazarus was a consequential stranger, one he thought was insignificant. What if he had behaved differently toward Lazarus during his lifetime when Lazarus was for him an angel, that is, one who carries a divine message? Now that he had learned the lesson, he wished for his brothers to recognize the significance of the stranger.

---

[1] Melinda Blau and Karen L. Fingerman demonstrated in their book, *Consequential Strangers*, W. W. Norton & Company, 2009.

Abraham told the rich man that his brothers would not listen even if one came back from the dead to warn them. The opportunities to hear the divine message are multiple. Often we miss the message, however, because we discount the messenger. The messenger might in fact be a consequential stranger, who has the power to change our life at least for the moment.

# Consider your
# Network of Consequential
# Strangers

Pick a day or two this week to try this exercise.

Keep a list of everyone you meet or talk with either face to face or via telephone, email, text or some other media. At the end of the day, look at your list noticing who of those people are family or friends. Who are strangers? Of what consequence in your life are these "strangers?" What contribution did they make to you or you to them?

Pick one name from your list of a person who most affected you emotionally. Was that person family, friend or stranger? Often people we considered insignificant or merely casual contacts turn out to be the ones who most affected us.

# Learn From
# Past Experience
# of Forgiveness

One time Jesus was eating at the house of a Pharisee. A woman brought some expensive oil and poured it on Jesus' feet. Some of the other guests objected. They thought such a use of the expensive oil was a waste. Besides, the people labeled her a "sinner." Jesus acknowledged many deeds she had done that missed the highest ideal. He did not apply the label to her. Not only that, he offered her forgiveness, a second chance, an opportunity to change and to grow into the image he held of her.

Jesus offers us the same opportunity, rooted in God's extravagant love for us. As we move into Jesus' ideal for us, we extend the same opportunity to others.

Reflect on a time when you have been able to successfully give another person a second chance. You can use your experience to lead you to another experience of offering forgiveness.

Look truthfully at one hurt you have been able to forgive. What steps did you take to get there— confess your contribution to a conflict, make amends, change behavior, let go of a label?

What feelings did you have to let go of—anger, denial, guilt, shame, or embarrassment?

Imagine what it would be like to live into forgiveness of another hurt.

# Meditate on the Fruits of the Spirit

Sitting quietly simply repeat the words of Paul's list of the fruits of the Spirit—love, joy, peace, patience, kindness, goodness, gentleness, faithfulness, self-control.

You could coordinate your repetitions with your breathing. On the in breath, say the word "love" and then repeat it again on the out breath. On the next in breath say the word "joy;" repeat it on the out breath. Do the same for each of the fruits of the Spirit.

# Offer a Blessing

Begin by asking for blessing for yourself: may I be happy; may I be free from suffering; may I have peace.

Extend the blessing to your family and friends. You can bless them in person or you can bring them into your imagination and bless them. May you be happy; may you be free from suffering; may you have peace.

Extend your blessing even further to those you don't know very well or maybe don't even know at all--a stranger on the street, a person you see in the newspaper or on the evening news.

Extend your blessing to those you think of as enemies. In so doing, you are practicing the teaching of Jesus: "Love your enemies, do good to those who hate you."

# Watch "I" and "We"
# Arise and Dissolve

Like waves of the ocean appear and dissolve back into the ocean so does our sense of self. When we are in a group, we experience the group as "we."

Next time you are in a group of people, look around at each person. What does it feel like to be "we" with this group? After you depart from the group, pause to ask, "What happened to the "we"?

Observing "we" leads to an obvious conclusion. The "we" dissolved when we departed. We could come back together. Even if we do come back together "we" will be different; we will be a new group, a different "we."

This experience helps you think about "I" in the second part of the practice. Just as the "we" changes, so "I" constantly changes. For most of us who think of ourselves as a constant, this is a bit more challenging to experience. Try it.

At a solitary moment, become aware of your "I." What are you aware of? Sometime later become aware of your "I" again. Are you aware of different things? What happened to the "I" in these two different experiences?

# Live in the Present Moment

This moment is the only moment.
It comes to you as a gift.
Savor it, treasure it.

You can practice this meditation following your breathing to celebrate the present moment.

On the in breath: I live in this moment.
On the out breath: The only moment.

On the in breath: I am aware of my body.*
On the out breath: I smile welcome and acceptance to my body.*

On the in breath: I live in this moment.
On the out breath: The only moment.

*In subsequent repetitions you can substitute emotions, feelings, thoughts, memories for body. For example, on the in breath you can say, "I am aware of my emotions." You can also name a specific emotion, a specific thought or memory, for instance, "I am aware that I'm thinking about my vacation." You can find many ways to modify this practice to fit the present moment of your own life and situation.

# Listen

Listening involves attention, being present, and hospitality. It is a highly valued skill among many people, including Native Americans. Listening involves "hearing the message," which may come by word, but more often by direct insight. During this week practice listening

- to yourself--listen especially to the sounds of your heart and your breathing. What do the sounds tell you about the sacredness of life?

- to other people--listen not only to the words; listen also to the feeling and the desires of another. What do you learn about the other person and about yourself?

- to creation--pay attention to creation. What sound do you most associate with what you see and feel? What is the message of the parts of creation you encountered this week?

# Look at the Stars

On a clear night look at the stars and dream. See if you agree with Vincent Van Gogh, "For my part I know nothing with any certainty, but the sight of the stars makes me dream."

As you gaze at the stars, what happens to you? What sensations and feelings do you experience? What thoughts and images arise?

# Let your Spending be
# your Thanksgiving

Next time you pay a bill and are tempted to grumble that you are spending your hard earned money, look at what you're paying for.  Say thank you.

You pay for groceries, "Thank for this food which nourishes me."

You pay your utility bills, "Thank you for heat, light and clean water."

You pay your taxes (ok this may be a little harder), "Thank you for the roads and schools, bridges and protection, and all the services the government provides."

# Random acts of Kindness

Kindness is contagious. See if you can perform one random act of kindness each day this week. If you miss a day, be kind to yourself and let it go!

Here are a couple of suggestions:

- Send a card or note to someone you think about.

- Buy a stranger a cup of coffee.

- Let someone go in front of you in the checkout line.

# Live Confidently

*You gain strength, courage, and confidence by every experience in which you really stop to look fear in the face. You are able to say to yourself, 'I lived through this horror. I can take the next thing that comes along.'* –Eleanor Roosevelt

Make a list of five times in your life when you have overcome an obstacle. For each event on your list ask yourself, what have I learned from that experience? And, how does that experience gives me confidence for whatever happens in my future?

# Live the Promise

I wrote this practice for the fourth Sunday of Easter, which is called Good Shepherd Sunday. In the readings for this day Jesus offers four promises:

My sheep hear my voice.

I know my sheep.

I give them eternal life.

No one will snatch them out of my hand.

Pick one of these phrases to live with for one day. You could try this four times using a different promise each day. Periodically through the day, stop what you're doing and repeat the words of the promise. What connections do you make? Do not judge whether they are logical; simply note the connection and go on. You may want to write about the connections you make in your journal.

You can practice this with other "promises" of your own choosing. Simply bring the promise into your awareness at various times in the day.

# ABOUT THE AUTHOR

Robert Flaherty, DMin, is a United Methodist clergyperson. He has served as pastor, district superintendent, Army and VA chaplain. He is author of numerous articles. He lives with his wife, Sandy, in Newberg, Oregon. He can be reached at drbobflaherty@gmail.com.

Made in the USA
Las Vegas, NV
13 December 2020